FUNKY MONKEY

written by

Melissa A. Towns

I would like to dedicate this book to my three sons
Kenigh, Kennedy and Kash.

Always remember by helping others,
they will be open to helping you.

Love always, Mommy.

This Book

Belongs To

_____

_____

Funky monkey was lying on the tree with his friends.

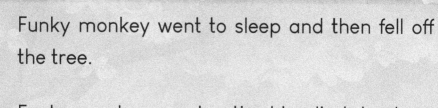

Funky monkey went to sleep and then fell off the tree.

Funky monkey was too tired to climb back up the tree, so he walked over to Elliot the alligator and asked if he could stand on his head so he could toss him back on the tree.

Elliot the alligator said, "Ok." When Funky Monkey went to stand on the alligator's head, he opened his mouth very wide and tried to eat him. Funky Monkey ran away holding his bottom.

Funky Monkey said, "I'll ask my friend, Leo the lion. Excuse me, Leo, I don't mean to bother you, but can you climb up the tree with me on your back so I can go back to sleep? I'm too tired to climb back up the tree."

The lion opened his mouth and roared very loudly that you can hear him from miles and miles away.

Funky Monkey was so scared, so he ran as fast as he could. While he was running, he tripped over his friend, George the giraffe, who was bent down eating.

Funky Monkey said, "Hey there, George, how are you?" George said, "I'm fine." Funky Monkey said, "Hey George, I need a huge favor." George said, "Sure. What do you need?"

"Can you give me a ride to that tree over there? I fell off the tree, and I'm too tired to climb back up the tree."

George the giraffe said, "Sure, no problem, but I need a favor from you." Funky Monkey said, "Sure. Whatever you need, George."

George said, "Can you pick up that branch and scratch my back for me while I'm giving you a ride back to the tree? My back has been itching all day and I just can't get to it." Funky monkey said, "Sure, George. No problem."

George the giraffe and Funky monkey arrived at the tree. George said, "We're here." George then raised his head and Funky Monkey walked to George's neck and then to the top of his head. Funky Monkey then hopped off the head of George the giraffe onto the branch of the tree where he was sleeping earlier.

Funky Monkey said,
"Thank you, George."

George said,
"Anytime, my friend!"

THE END

CPSIA information can be obtained
at www.ICGtesting.com
Printed in the USA
LVHW050600100921
697443LV00007B/331